How to Write a Short Book
That Will Sell Forever

RICHARD FENTON &
ANDREA WALTZ

Published by

SUCCESS IN

PAGES
SHORT BOOKS. BIG IDEAS.

ISBN 978-1-947814-94-3

Copyright © February 2019

All rights reserved.

Except as permitted under the United States Copyright Act of 1976, no part of this publication may be reproduced or distributed in any form or by any means, or stored in a data retrieval system, without the written permission of the publisher.

One book can change everything.

Interested in writing a book of your own?

Get our <u>FREE</u> checklist covering every step of the writing, publishing and book marketing process at:

<u>MillionDollarBookFormula.com</u>

"I do believe something very magical can happen when you read a good book."

-J.K. Rowling

"Something very magical can happen when you write one, too."

-Richard Fenton & Andrea Waltz

INTRODUCTION

Los Angeles, October 2003

We're huddled over the fax machine, waiting for our lives to change.

Our agent had gotten us a publishing deal with the biggest New York publisher you can think of—seriously, think of the biggest publisher you can, and that's who was going to publish our book! After some back and forth, the publisher said they'd be faxing over an offer the next morning at 10 a.m.

So, there we were, the two of us—standing shoulder-to-shoulder over the fax machine... waiting... waiting...

And nothing arrived.

Finally, we called our agent, who said, "I'll call you back in five minutes." Another excruciating hour later, our agent called back.

The news wasn't good.

"It looks like they decided to pull the plug on the deal," the agent said flatly.

We were flabbergasted. "What? How could that be? You said it was a done deal! How could this happen?"

The agent explained that the publisher had their marketing department do a projection of how many books they thought we'd sell. The conclusion was there wouldn't be enough demand for a highly niched, targeted book like ours.

On top of that, they decided our platform—the number of people we had on our mailing list and the number of speaking engagements we were delivering—wasn't big enough. "They determined your book would be lucky to sell 5,000 copies," the agent said. "They're out."

"So who do we go to next?" we asked.

"There is no next," the agent said. "When the biggest publisher in New York says a book won't sell, it won't sell. We're done."

The phone line went dead, and that was it—our dream of being traditionally published authors was over.

After the shock of losing what was a "done deal" had passed, we had a decision to make. The biggest decision of our careers. Do we take their word for it that our book wouldn't sell? Or should we soldier on, marketing *"Go for No!"*® as a self-published book?

The answer wasn't as difficult as we thought it would be. Of course we were going to press forward. After all, we'd spent a lot of time and money already. Abandoning our "child" was unthinkable.

Fast Forward 15 Years...

The little book the big publisher said would never sell more than 5,000 copies has sold in excess of 400,000 copies, reached #1 on two Amazon sub-lists, gathered over 1,000 5-star reviews, and has been translated into nine languages. More importantly, the book continues to sell extremely well two decades after we wrote it—and a full decade after we finally placed it on Amazon in April of 2007.

The Best Part Is, We Aren't Special

The best part of our story is that we aren't special—we're normal people, just like you. We had no big starting warchest or inheritance. No special connections in publishing. We were just two wannabe authors with the dream to write a book, start our own business, and take control of our lives.

And the success we've enjoyed wasn't the result of chance or luck. We didn't get "hit by lightning." What we accomplished was *mostly* planned, was *reasonably* predictable, and is *generally* reproducible.

There *is* a formula, as it turns out.

About the Title of This Book

When we first decided to do this book, we came up with a list of titles, which we showed to friends and business associates for their opinions. This got us down to two titles.

The next step was to have those two titles formally tested. *Million Dollar Book Formula* was the clear winner.

There were a few people who—though they liked the title—questioned whether it was really possible to make a million dollars with a book. The answer is, *yes*.

For people who want the numbers:

- *Some books were sold back-of-room at speaking engagements for the full $12 cover price.*

- *Many, many copies have been sold through Amazon over the last 10 years, with royalties in the $5-7 range.*

- *Others were sold "in bulk" to corporate clients, with prices ranging from $6-10 per copy, depending on the size of the order.*

- *Still more books were sold to book clubs and wholesalers, with royalties ranging between $1-3 per copy (after cost of printing).*

To make the math easy, taking our total units sold (400,000) multiplied by an average of $5 profit per book, it doesn't take a rocket scientist to see it's not only possible to earn a million dollars with a book... *we did it.*

To be clear, we're not suggesting that everyone reading this book will be able to duplicate our success. And not everyone who writes a book—even if they follow the formula laid out in the pages to follow—will have the tenacity to stay at it the way we have.

Then There's the "Back End" Business Part of the Equation

Beyond the money an author can make with a book, there's also the income that can be created by building a "back end business" around the book—we're talking, speaking, coaching, consulting, online courses, etc.—and on and on. For most people, this is where the long-term money really is.

(<u>Note</u>: We'll talk more about this later.)

Now, About the Subtitle

Truth be told, we grappled more over the subtitle *(How to Write a Short Book That Will Sell Forever)* than we did over the title itself. The issue we had is with the word "*write.*"

The word *write* could possibly lead some people into thinking this book is *literally* about the art of writing: *you know, first-person versus third person, sentence structure, character development, and the like.* It is not.

The Million Dollar Book Formula covers none of those things. So, if that's what you were looking for, we apologize.

Our book is about the process of finding a problem that needs to be solved, providing solutions, and then promoting what you've written for as long as it takes to get traction in the marketplace.

If *that* happens to be of interest, keep reading.

You won't be disappointed.

Finally, A Few Assumptions

To make the most of the time we have together on the pages to follow, we are going to make a few assumptions:

1. *You are pre-sold on the value of writing a book. So we are not going to spend much time "selling" you on all the wonderful reasons why being an author and having a book is a great move. We know you have your reasons (which we will address in a bit), and that is great!*

2. *You are interested in writing a non-fiction book. If you are writing an autobiography or fiction book, there are a ton of books that are a better fit in helping you with those categories.*

3. *You understand that a book is one piece in your overall puzzle. In other words, you have some kind of business mission that a book can help you grow.*

4. *You know a bit about the "self-publishing" model and understand you can DIY as opposed to trying to get a big New York publisher to publish your book, and that it is possible to be wildly successful without having to rely on a publisher at all.*

Okay, with these assumptions established, let's begin.

THE CASE FOR SHORT BOOKS

So, how did we go from standing over the fax machine and not getting the big, life-changing offer—feeling devastated and depressed—to selling 400,000 copies of the book we were assured by the "experts" would never sell 5,000 copies?

Well, there was no silver bullet that led to our book's success. It was a series of small things that, when added together, made the difference. And the first one may surprise you.

It was page count.

Yes, we're saying that the number of pages in our book played a significant part in the book's success—more specifically, the *limited* number of pages. You see, our book was only 80 pages in length.

As much as we'd love to take credit for being smart enough to recognize how important the size of the book would be to its success, we really can't. The truth is, we kept the book short because we were self-publishing and wanted to keep the costs down.

We also wanted to give away copies to decision makers who might want to buy books for sales teams. And we knew it also costs three times more to ship a 250-page book than an 80-page book because postage is based on weight.

We didn't have the money to make it longer—which turned out to be a big positive, not a negative.

So a short book it *had* to be.

People Want Short Books

What we learned over time was that people wanted short books—especially busy business people—which explains why some of the biggest bestsellers of all time are very short.

For example:

- Napoleon Hill's *"Think and Grow Rich"* is just 104 pages.

- *"The One Minute Manager"* by Ken Blanchard and Spencer Johnson is 112 pages.

- Og Mandino's *"The Greatest Salesman in the World"* is a whopping 128 pages.

- *"Who Moved My Cheese"* by Spencer Johnson is a mere 95 pages.

- And *"Jonathan Livingston Seagull"* by Richard Bach (which happens to be one of the cleverest "motivational" books ever written) is only 95 pages.

The five books above have sold a combined 200 million copies. So far. Even decades after publication, they *continue* to sell millions of copies per year.

Most Books Are Too Damn Big

One of our favorite short books is *"Love Yourself"* by Kamal Ravikant, which is a mere 60 pages in length. When it arrived, I (Richard) read it in less than 45 minutes, then proceeded to sit in the office across from Andrea and read it again, aloud this time. *That's two cover-to-cover reads of a book in less than two hours!*

Why is that a big deal? Simple. Because there are millions of books sold every year that never even get started, let alone finished. Because they're just too damn big.

Here's what another of our favorite authors, James Altucher, said about "*Love Yourself*":

> *"Kamal did something that ZERO publishers would say 'yes' to. He wrote and published a 70-page book. Publishers hate 70-page books. For them a book is a strict 60,000-80,000 words... not 10,000 words. But Kamal proved them wrong. 2,300 positive reviews later he proved them VERY wrong. It's one of the most inspirational books ever written. For me, Kamal changed the definition of what a book is and could be. It could be small. It could be big, too. It could be whatever you want."*

Consumption Is the Key to Word-of-Mouth Advertising

Now, maybe you're thinking: *Who cares? If someone wants to buy my book and not read it, what difference does it make? They paid for it, right? Isn't that what matters?*

No.

If you want to sell books—lots and lots of books—people need to do more than *buy* your book. They need to *read* your book.

You see:

- *People don't recommend movies they haven't seen...*

- *People don't recommend restaurants they've never eaten in...*

- *And they don't recommend books they haven't read!*

Keeping a book short triples the chances people will actually read it...*and then tell others about it.* That's where word-of-mouth advertising comes from—from people telling other people about something they've *experienced,* something they've *consumed.*

Thinking the key to success is merely getting people to *buy* your book is short-sighted. You have two goals:

1. Get people to *buy* your book.

2. Get people to *consume* your book.

And when it comes to books, size and consumption are directly related. Think about all the books you have on your bookshelf right now that you keep telling yourself, *"One of these days I'm going to tackle that book."* But you still haven't. Why? Chances are good that it's just too big.

Page Length is Dropping, Radically

There are exceptions, of course. There are many big books that reach bestseller status, so we're not saying that a book *must* be short to be successful—only that they *can* be. But the trend is definitely moving toward shorter, not longer.

For example: According to research done by bestselling author Tucker Max, the average page length of every New

York Times #1 Non-Fiction Bestseller has fallen steadily since 2011:

- In 2011, the average length peaked at 467 pages.

- By 2013, the size had fallen to 367 pages.

- In 2015, the page count was down to 345.

- Then, in 2017, the average length fell dramatically to just 273 pages!

As if all this isn't proof enough about the rising popularity of small books (or "short reads" as Amazon refers to them), consider the growing popularity of book summaries:

- *"The 10x Rule"* by Grant Cardone is 240 pages... *with a 64-page summary available on Amazon.*

- *"The 5 Dysfunctions of a Team"* by Patrick Lencioni is 229 pages...*with a 76-page summary.*

- *"The 5 Second Rule"* by Mel Robbins is 240 pages in length...*with a summary at 89 pages.*

- And you can buy a 102-page summary of Tim Ferris' *"Tribe of Mentors"* (one of our favorite books, even if it is a whopping 624 pages).

What's interesting is that no one has ever done a summary "knock-off" of *"Go for No!"* After all, who bothers to knock off an 80-page book?

Interestingly, the two comments we've heard most often over the years about *"Go for No!"* are:

1. *"This is a great book!"*
2. *"Thanks for keeping it short!"*

Which was funny, because when we decided to go forward with a book of just 80-pages, we were a little concerned it was too short for the marketplace. As it turned out, the book's length wasn't a drawback at all. It was actually one of the book's greatest assets. In fact, the length of our book actually became part of our marketing—a selling point.

Once we started hearing people say how happy they were with the length of the book, we'd mail it to decision makers with a note that said, *"Take this book on your next flight with you. It's a great airplane read."*

That was it. The book did the rest, driving bulk order sales and speaking engagements—*because it got read.* Make no mistake, the marketplace is changing—*and short is where it's going.*

THE SEARCH FOR A SUCCESS "FORMULA"

Our book, *"Go for No!"* hit #1 on the Amazon Sales & Selling list for the first time on New Year's Eve, 2010. We remember it because we were living in a vacation rental in South Beach to see if we liked Florida enough to move there permanently. We looked at the computer screen late in the afternoon and saw we'd reached the top spot.

That night we went to a great dinner to celebrate, then sat on the stone walkway along Collins Avenue and watched fireworks at midnight. It was a moment we'll never forget.

This is not to say that we're geniuses—it had, through trial and error (a lot of error), taken us years to move *"Go for No!"* up the charts. Also, we'd written other books along the way, and none of them were as successful. Far from it, in fact.

So we found ourselves wondering: *"Why did 'Go for No!' do so well, yet our other books performed so poorly?"* It was a question that nagged us constantly. After all, if we were smart enough to make one book a bestseller, why couldn't we do the same thing with the others?

That's when we got a call from our friend, Patrick Galvin.

Patrick Galvin is a professional speaker who'd just finished writing a business book called, *"The Connector's Way,"* and wanted to know if we'd be willing to read it before it went to print.

After reading the book, we gave Patrick our feedback. A year later, Patrick sent us this testimonial:

> *"This past year, we sold over 10,000 copies of "The Connector's Way," received 184 reviews on Amazon (93 percent of which are 5-star) and the book has served as the launch-off point for a six-figure speaking career. I shudder to think about how things might have turned out without Richard and Andrea's advice."*

Needless to say, we were very happy for our friend and glad our feedback had made a positive impact, but it got us to wondering:

> *Why were we able to look at Patrick's book and see the things that could and should be better with such clarity—yet not figure out why some of our books had failed so miserably? Were we too close to our own work to be objective? Or was it something else?*

We needed to find out.

The Search for "The Formula" Was On

So, we decided to study not only our books but many of the best-sellers over the last 50-plus-years to see if we could come up with a reliable, predictable "formula" that explained why some of our books sold and others didn't. We wanted to *crack the code,* so to speak.

We rented a vacation house in the mountains of the Shenandoah Valley in Virginia—and because we were 100 percent committed to our project, we rented the house for three months. So it was ninety days in the mountains with nothing to do but focus on why some of our books sold, and others didn't.

Well, do that—and drink wine!

We were about halfway into our retreat, working our way through thousands of pages of information on writing and publishing books, and we weren't getting anywhere. The information was good, but none of it directly answered our question.

We were getting frustrated.

Admittedly, the three-month getaway was nice, but if we went back to Orlando without achieving what we'd set out to do, we would have considered the mission a failure.

Then, one day, we ventured down the mountain to do our weekly food shop. And that's when the answer came, at the least likely of moments—in the form of a question—standing in the condiment aisle at the Martin's grocery store in Harrisonburg, Virginia.

> *What if we'd been going about this book thing all wrong? What if instead of studying the way authors and publishers market books, we studied how major corporations marketed their products? Companies like Proctor & Gamble®, Ford®, Budweiser® and Nike®. What if we put the book question aside and focused on how the biggest and most successful corporations in the world created products and built their brands to sell well over a long period of time?*

So that's what we did.

The 13 "Success Ingredients"

When we were done, we'd discovered 13 specific things that, collectively, created the greatest chance for any product or service to achieve lasting success.

And yet, the big question remaining: Would the success ingredients apply equally well to books?

The answer was, yes.

Not only did the 13 Success Ingredients apply to books, but when we referenced them against the books we'd written, we found that the books that had sold well had most, if not all, of the ingredients—while the books that had failed had fewer than half.

When we packed up the car two months later for the trip back to Florida, we'd achieved what we'd set out to do.

We'd discovered the formula.

And here it is:

13 SUCCESS INGREDIENTS™

Success Ingredient #1:
PURPOSE

Success Ingredient #7:
PLACEMENT

Success Ingredient #2:
PROBLEM

Success Ingredient #8:
PROMOTION

Success Ingredient #3:
PROSPECTS

Success Ingredient #9:
PLATFORM

Success Ingredient #4:
PRODUCT

Success Ingredient #10:
PARTNERSHIPS

Success Ingredient #5:
PACKAGING

Success Ingredient #11:
PROGRESSION

Success Ingredient #6:
PRICING

Success Ingredient #12:
PROTECTION

Success Ingredient #13:
PERSISTENCE

MillionDollarBookFormula.com

Offering "Proof"

Now, this all looks good on paper, but you're probably wondering: *Does the formula presented in this book really work?* More importantly, will it work for *you*?

It's one thing for us to tell you the *"Million Dollar Book Formula"* works... *that you should simply trust us.* This is *our* book, after all. It contains *our* concepts and philosophies. What else are we supposed to say?

So we knew that most people reading this book would want more than our word. *We'd need to provide proof.*

Once we finished our research and finalized the formula, the first thing we did was analyze our previous books—the best sellers and not-so-bestsellers—to see how they matched up.

We were blown away:

- *"Go for No!,"* which has sold 400,000 copies and reached #1 numerous times on various Amazon bestseller sub-list categories, had all 13 of the success ingredients going for it.

- *"Retail Magic,"* our next bestseller with over 40,000 copies sold, had eight of the 13 Success Ingredients.

- *"Sales Safari,"* our third bestseller (a 64-page short book we'd published during our early years consulting for the retail industry), hit 7 of the 13 success ingredients.

- *"Million Dollar Year,"* our fifth best-selling book, hit only six of the 13 ingredients

- *"Fear Factory,"* the next book in line in terms of sales, included only 5 of the 13 ingredients.

And our biggest disappointment of all, *"What Would Lincoln Say?"*—a book we'd released with great fanfare, sold so poorly we literally had 7,500 copies taken to a book recycler—had only three of the 13!

Putting the Formula to the Ultimate Test

Next, we decided to put our money where our mouths were by publishing someone else's book—a book that didn't have our names on the cover—and apply every one of the 13 Success Ingredients to the writing, publishing and marketing process.

The book we published was *"Freakishly Effective Social Media for Network Marketing"* by Ray and Jessica Higdon, and results speak for themselves. *"Freakishly Effective Social Media for Network Marketing"*:

- Reached #1 on Amazon's *"Multi-Level Marketing"* bestseller list.

- It also hit #1 on Amazon's *"Home-Based Business"* bestseller list.

- It hit #1 on Amazon's prestigious *"Movers & Shakers"* list.

- It climbed all the way to #93 on Amazon's *"Overall Bestseller"* list.

- And, as of this writing, *"Freakishly Effective Social Media for Network Marketing"* has 427 reviews, 97 percent being 5-star (with the vast majority of those reviews coming from Verified Purchasers).

Most importantly, perhaps, is that the book is still among the top-20 bestsellers in every one of these categories... *six months after it was first published.*

We don't tell you any of this to brag. We tell you this only to provide proof that the formula works. And we'd be remiss if we didn't point out that Ray and Jessica Higdon have a decent-sized email list and are extremely active on social media. As such, if you haven't started building your author platform, then get busy building one.

But that was the point of our mission: to find a formula for writing and marketing books that was predictably successful—one that didn't require luck to work, or for the Book Gods to intervene on your behalf.

Don't get us wrong—*luck* is a good thing—as is having the Book Gods smile down upon you. But *luck* is not a *plan.* Neither is *prayer.* What if the Book Gods are tied up helping Stephen King put out another bestseller?

No, you need a *process* you can count on: *a formula.*

And here it is.

SUCCESS INGREDIENT #1:
PURPOSE

One of the most well-known problem-solving and planning approaches ever created is the *"Who? What? Where? When? Why?"* method (or *5Ws Method,* for short.)

The problem with the *5Ws* Method is that the most important question isn't up front where it should be.

- *Before the who...*
- *Before the what...*
- *Before the where...*
- *Before the when...*

The first question should always be...

Why?

Major organizations always know the why *(or, in other words, the purpose)* for creating a new product. Ninety-nine times out of 100, it's to generate a profit and return for their shareholders. They may fail, but their goal—*their why*—is always clear.

It's to make money.

Authors rarely start with such focused clarity. They *think* they're clear on the reason they're writing a book, but they're not. Or they start with a *bag of reasons,* some of which are in direct conflict with each other.

For example, here are 20 reasons *why* someone might decide to write a book:

1. *To make money.*

2. *To check writing a book off their bucket list.*

3. *Because they have a story they feel they must tell.*

4. *To leave the book as a history for their grandchildren to read someday.*

5. *To provide people with a solution to a problem.*

6. *To inspire people and make a difference in the world.*

7. *To impress their friends and family.*

8. *To start a career as an author or use a book as a way to make a career change.*

9. *To see their name on the cover.*

10. *To gain prestige by winning a contest or literary prize.*

11. *To use the book as a business card for marketing a product or service, or to launch a career as a professional speaker or trainer.*

12. *To establish an aura of celebrity around their name.*

13. *To honor a relative by writing their biography.*

14. *To enhance their credibility by putting the words "Bestselling Author of..." after their name.*

15. *To establish themselves as an expert on a specific topic.*

16. *To give the book away as a lead-magnet to build an email list.*

17. *To start a movement.*

18. *To attract media attention.*

19. *Because they're bored and need something to do.*

20. *Because everyone else is doing it, they figure, "Hey, why not me?"*

We've probably missed about 50 other reasons why someone might write a book, but this list is a good start.

Here's the thing: No book will do all of the things on the list above. In fact, few books will ever achieve half of these things.

You want to write a book about your Aunt Margaret's journey to America in the 1960s? Go ahead, have at it.

We're sure she'll love it. But don't be surprised when it doesn't sell. Item #13 on the list will rarely (if ever) achieve item #1.

On the other hand, if you write a killer book on overcoming sales objections, there's a good chance your book will sell, assuming you promote it effectively. But there's also a good chance Aunt Margaret will hate it.

Don't get us wrong. All the items on the list are valid reasons for writing a book...*but your book can't achieve them all.*

No book ever does.

Most of the books we've written, especially the ones that underperformed, were started because we had a *flash of inspiration*—often nothing more than what we thought was a great title—and we were off and running (or writing, as it were.)

You must know the *why* (the *purposeful expectation* of your book) <u>before</u> you start writing. In other words, *"think before you ink."*

For the purposes of this book, we're going to assume your primary motivation is #1 on the list—to make money with your book. You were, after all, attracted to the words "million" and "dollar" in the title.

SUCCESS INGREDIENTS #2 and #3:
PROBLEM & PROSPECTS

The key to <u>all</u> successful products and services is that they solve a problem of some kind.

- *Laundry detergent solves the problem of getting dirt and stains out of dirty clothes.*

- *Cars solve the problem of getting around.*

- *Water solves the problem of thirst and hydration; cola solves the problem of thirst and flavor; diet cola solves the problem of drinking cola with too many calories in it.*

- *Restaurants solve the problem of cooking and then having to clean your own dishes.*

- *A pen solves the problem of needing to write something down, so you can access the information at a later date.*

And this problem/solution idea is present in every book you've ever read, whether it's a non-fiction how-to book or a pure entertainment thriller novel.

In our case (with *"Go for No!"*), the problem was the fear of failure and rejection: a big problem with near universal appeal because the people who had the problem were acutely aware of it, and in many cases, were actively searching for a solution. This was in direct opposition to our other books.

Our other books—the ones that underperformed—while well-written (at least we think so), did not solve a problem. People enjoyed them. They got good reviews. But they didn't solve a serious problem. And to the degree to which they *did* solve a problem, the problem wasn't acute enough and/or the number of prospects who wanted that problem solved was too limited.

For a book to sell well, especially over a long period of time, it's got to solve a problem for which there are:

- *A significant number of people who have a problem...*
- *Know they have the problem...*
- *And, ideally, are actively searching for a solution to the problem.*

For example, imagine a book titled: *"The Art of the Long Business Meeting."* Who has this problem? Virtually no one. Generally speaking, people hate business meetings— so the chances that someone is searching for a book that will tell them to have more of them in some better way is nonexistent.

Whereas the formula for writing a successful book is somewhat complicated, the formula for a book that will fail is fairly simple:

No Problem + No Prospects = No Sales.

No One Really Wants to Buy Your Book

One time we conducted a *"Go for No!"* workshop for a company that had done a bulk purchase of the book for everyone in attendance. The program went well and at the end of the day, we asked the VP of Sales, the man who had hired us, how he felt about the workshop. His answer really took us aback. He said:

> *"It doesn't matter how I feel about your workshop or your book. I didn't hire you because I wanted a workshop or a book—both of them take up lots of our people's time. What I want is for the problem to go away. Hell, you could run around the room and sprinkle pixie dust over everyone and if their fears of failure and rejection go away, it would be a bargain."*

We came away from that experience realizing he was right. No one was buying our book because they wanted our book. They wanted their problem solved. Period. The book was simply a means to an end.

Provide a "Positive Change of State"

One of the great myths perpetually put forward is the one that suggests "people hate change." In reality, people are desperate for a *change of state* in their lives—as long as the change involved is perceived as positive. When offered the chance to move from a negative state to a positive state, most people say, *"Heck, yeah! Sign me up!"* This is especially true if the positive change is in one of the following five areas:

- *Health*
- *Wealth*
- *Relationships*
- *Success*
- *Happiness*

The vast majority of bestselling *non-fiction* books involve a change in state—from a negative to a positive—in the area of these five human wants.

What Problem Does Fiction Solve?

The surface-level answer is *entertainment*. But entertainment is not the problem—*entertainment is the solution*. The problem is the core human need for temporary escape.

By its very nature, escapism is the removal of a negative state—worry, sadness, boredom, whatever—that's the problem. Which explains why billions of dollars are spent each year on movies, concerts, theater tickets, sporting events, etc. They are all, at their core, forms of *escape*.

Are There Already Books on Your Topic Area?

A really good question to ask before writing any book is: *Are there already books on this topic?* Seems logical enough, right? Here's what you probably don't expect: The answer you're looking for is...

YES.

When we first started, we thought that competition was going to be our biggest problem. There were already books written on our subject. We also assumed writing a book on an original idea was the key to success. We were wrong.

When it comes to writing a book, originality is highly overrated. In fact, the opposite is true. You do not want a completely unique idea because if you do, you'll have a hard time finding prospects.

During my early years in the National Speaker's Association, I (Richard) had the good future to meet a woman named Dottie Walters. Dottie was a professional speaker, a legend in the industry, really. She was also the founder of the Walter's International Speaker's Bureau.

One day, after one of the local chapter meetings, I approached Dottie and asked for her advice regarding finding a topic to speak and write on. Dottie looked me straight in the eye and said: *"You only have two choices, Richard. The first choice is to say something new—something no one has ever said before. Or, two, say something old that everyone has already heard but say it in a new and different way."*

Then Dottie added...

"By the way, there is nothing new."

In retrospect, it was the best advice I've ever gotten.

For example: *Is there a need for another Italian restaurant in your city?* The initial answer for most people is usually, *no*—there are already 12 Italian restaurants in a five-mile radius of where you live.

But what if we change the question to: *"Is there a need for another <u>really great</u> Italian restaurant in your city?"* The answer to this question is almost always, yes.

In our case, with *"Go for No!"*, the fact that hundreds of books have been written on overcoming failure and rejection was a very good thing. It meant there were a lot of people with the problem. The only things that mattered was our ability to write a different book—ideally a better book—with a great title that made it stand out from the crowd.

Oh, and consider this...

When we set out to write *this* book—the one you're reading right this very second—we knew there were already hundreds of books on the topic. Which is wonderful, because it means there is a problem to be solved and people who are searching for solutions.

Check—and *check*.

SUCCESS INGREDIENT #4:
PRODUCT

You could make the case that every element of a book is *the product*. However, when you think about it—just like buying a bottle of detergent—the *product* and its *packaging* are two very different things.

In the case of detergent, the liquid that gets poured in the washing machine is the product. Everything else—the paper label and the plastic bottle the liquid comes in—is packaging: a delivery system with promises printed on it.

In the case of books:

- The <u>PRODUCT</u> is made up of words and pictures—the value they have, both in terms of the immediate emotional reaction for the reader, as well as the lasting impact on the reader's life.

- The <u>PACKAGING</u> of the book is comprised of the cover—the title, cover art, the book's "trim size," the book description, etc. The book's packaging is <u>not</u> the product.

For the purposes of this chapter, we're talking about the *inside* of the book—the actual content that provides the promised solution to the problem being addressed.

Don't get us wrong: the outside of your book is important, too—critical, in fact. Because the packaging is what gets the product (book) sold, started and read. It's just that we're not dealing with the packaging here. That will be covered in the next Success Ingredient. Right now we're focused on the words.

The Quality of the Content/Writing Matters

There are some people who will tell you the "writing" doesn't matter much anymore—that the key to success is in pumping out tons of content. *"Quantity is more important than quality,"* they say. They are *wrong*.

Does this mean you have to be a great writer to write a great book?

No.

Many of the best-selling non-fiction books of all time have been written by people who were not *writers* by trade. They were experts on a specific topic who had a passion for their message and took the time to craft an understandable solution. The writing itself wasn't great, but the solution to the problem was.

Besides, you can get help with the writing from various types of editors and, if necessary, a ghost writer. And while editing and ghost writing requires time and money, so does producing a crappy product.

The quality of the writing impacts:

- *The reader experience...*
- *Understanding of the content...*
- *Book reviews...*
- *Book returns...*
- *Kindle Unlimited page reads...*
- *Word-of-mouth sales...*
- *The likelihood of bulk orders...*
- *The sales of your next book (and your book/books after that)*

In any case, do not listen to people who tell you the writing isn't important.

Reducing the Theme to a Single Sentence

Once you've decided on the problem you're attempting to solve, it's helpful to reduce the overall theme of the book to a single sentence—and not necessarily the book's title, though this may sometimes be the case.

To do this, imagine you told someone you were writing a book, and they asked, *"Oh, what's it about?"* Think of it like an elevator pitch, only shorter. Instead of 30 seconds, you only had five seconds. What would you say?

Why is this important? Well, it's not so you can explain what your book is about to people in elevators (though this ability will come in handy later). It's for the purposes of staying focused while *writing* the book.

- *It's to explain your book to yourself.*

- *It's to create focused clarity around what your book is about...and what it isn't about.*

- *It's to define the parameters of what is going to go in the book...and what is not.*

Here are several examples of reducing an entire book's message down to a single sentence:

- <u>Book</u>: *"Jab, Jab, Jab, Right Hook: How to Tell Your Story in a Noisy Social World"* by Gary Vaynerchuk

- <u>Single Sentence Summary</u>: *How to give value first so people will be eager to help you later.*

- <u>Book</u>: *"The Miracle Morning: The Not-So-Obvious Secret Guaranteed to Transform Your Life Before 8 AM"* by our friend, Hal Elrod

- <u>Single Sentence Summary</u>: *Specific things to do every morning that will make your entire day (and life) a success.*

- <u>Book</u>: *"The War of Art"* by Stephen Pressfield

- <u>Single Sentence Summary</u>: *How to overcome your mind's resistance to finish your creative project.*

(Note: The single sentence summaries above are our takes on each book's theme, not necessarily the author's.)

Here's the single-sentence summary we used while writing *"Go for No!"* is:

> *"Change the way people think about failure and rejection to increase their success.*

This clarity helped us make sure we stayed on point. For example, it was very tempting to include a chapter on how to convince a gatekeeper to say "yes" to get in to see the boss. And as tempted as we were to include a chapter on *overcoming objections*, we didn't. Not because those aren't important topics—they are. It's just that those are *go for yes* strategies. Our book wasn't called, *"Go for Yes."*

It was *"Go for No!"*

Trust us: If you don't have a clear idea of the parameters and the purpose of your book *before* you write it, there's a good chance your book will lose its focus and end up going all over the place.

Maybe that's why most books are too big.

Go Heavy on Stories, Examples and Analogies

"But I don't have any stories!" We hear authors say this too often during our *"Million Dollar Book Formula"* coaching sessions. And it's never true. Everyone has stories. It's just that most people haven't taken the time to mine them.

Stories are the glue that holds a good book together. And a good movie. Or play. Or speech. Our history as human beings on Earth is merely a collection of stories. As such, stories are the single greatest tool in an author's success tool kit.

So, how do you figure out what your stories are? Well, let us tell you a *story* about that!

Early in our careers, we hired a speaker/marketing consultant to work with us on the direction our business would take. Her name was Juanelle Teague, and she worked as a booking agent for Zig Ziglar for many years.

One of the exercises Juanelle encouraged us to do was to take a stack of index cards and write down the key events of our life, one event per card, starting from the age of two, all the way to the present. What kind of events? Large events and small events. Funny events and sad, soul-crushing events. Anything and everything that came to mind, she told us to write it down.

When we were done, we had a stack of over 100 cards. More important, we've used the stories mined during those two days with Juanelle for almost 15-years. Whenever we're looking for something to talk or write about, we go back to the story cards we created.

Now, this is not to say that every chapter of your book has to be peppered with stories, though some people do exactly that and do it very effectively. In any case, a few well-placed personal stories in your book will:

- *Make people think*
- *Connect you to the reader*
- *Provide "Ah ha!" moments*
- *Make people feel they know you*
- *Keep your book from being "dry" or boring*

- *Make your book memorable and "sticky"*
- *Provide real-world examples of the points you're making*

And, perhaps more than anything, well-told stories stimulate emotion.

Make Them Laugh, Cry, and Reflect

Never underestimate the impact value of making people laugh, cry, reflect or all of the above. Before including a story, you need to ask yourself:

- *Is this story relevant to the content being covered?*
- *Does it provide clarity and drive home the point you're trying to make?*
- *Does the story have the power to touch the reader's emotions?*
- *Will the story make the point—or perhaps the entire book—more memorable?*

If the answers are *yes*, then by all means, put in the story. If the answers are *no*, then you probably shouldn't.

Include Your Personality and "Unique Point of View"

Make sure that whatever you write includes your personality and your unique point-of-view.

As we mentioned earlier, the topic of your book has probably been written on before—at least some version of it—and that's a good thing. *But even though it's been done before, it's never been done by you.*

- *Not with your stories...*
- *And not from your unique point-of-view...*
- *And with your personality.*

Not only do your stories and your unique point-of-view differentiate you from everyone else, they're also the hardest things for other people to duplicate and steal.

A good example is the book, *"Get Over Your Damn Self,"* by Romi Neustadt. When you look at her reviews, you'll see numerous comments about how down-to-earth Romi is...and how funny and real she is...and how she's not one to sugar coat stuff.

The same is true for the book, *Girlboss,* a business memoir that comes across as extremely real and authentic.

Infuse who you are into your book. Be yourself and be bold.

Quality Control...AKA "Editing"

For some products, they have inspectors, or testers. In the book world, they have editors. But you might think, do I really need a professional editor? There are two answers to this question:

- The first answer is: YES.
- The second answer is: ALWAYS.

A clean text, free of mistakes, is not one of a book's benefits as far as a reader is concerned—it's a minimum expectation. The good news is, like everything else today, there are people who are out there you can hire on a freelance basis to edit your book.

The three types of editors are:

1. **Developmental Editor**

   Also known as a "content editor" a developmental editor does the substantive, major edits of a book's text. A content editor will delete, move and/or reorganize text, and potentially make suggestions for adding content where it's needed to create clarity.

2. **Copy-Editor**

   Also known as a "line editor", a copy editor will address issues with spelling, punctuation, grammar. And they may make some content and style comments along the way, though this is not their primary function. Lastly, there's the...

3. **Proofreader**

   Proofreading, which involves looking for typos, repeated words, missed words, and the like, is the most basic and least expensive service of the three. It's the final step, *after* your Developmental Editor (if you're using one) and your Line Editor do their work.

Think of the three editors as going from *big* adjustments, to *medium-sized* adjustments, and then small corrections.

Here's the good news. Unless you really struggle with organizing your thoughts (and writing in general), you most likely will not need a Content Editor. But no matter how good you think you are, you absolutely must hire a decent Line Editor and a very good, detail-oriented Proofreader. A poorly edited book is guaranteed to generate bad reviews, which is something you absolutely do not want.

Quality Control...AKA "Editing"

Yes. Even if you know what you're doing, *you* can read and edit your book a 100 times yourself, and it still won't be enough. Why? Because the person doing the editing is *you*. The concepts you thought were explained so perfectly? A fresh set of eyes will show you where you were wrong, where you missed the mark.

And you can proofread your manuscript until the cows come home (a saying we admit we don't fully understand but seems appropriate here) and still not catch every error because you are the one who mizpelled the word in the first place (yes, that was a joke).

And just so you know: Your proofreader will miss some things, too—they are human, after all. But he or she is going to do a better job than you will, guaranteed.

The good news is, if your errors are small enough—and your book content is good enough—people will look right past them and not even notice. And as Grant Cardone is famous for saying, *"It's better to be a best-selling author than it is to be a best-writing author."*

SUCCESS INGREDIENT #5:
PACKAGING

Because we were so optimistic that *"Go for No!"* was going to sell—and because the cost-per-book went down dramatically if we ordered a large quantity—we did an initial print-run of 10,000 copies.

Once the books arrived, we mailed 500 copies to decision makers and book reviewers, an effort that was received with a resounding...THUD!!! There was literally no response. Nothing. *Crickets.* We couldn't understand it. Somehow, we'd missed the mark.

Then we figured it out. The books must not have been delivered. Some disgruntled postal-worker must have tossed our bulk book mailing into the trash dumpster, probably because they were too lazy to process and deliver it. That had to be it!

Then we got our first (and only) order from the mailing.

We were wrong: The books *had* been delivered. Our hearts sank. We had 9,500 copies stacked in the garage...and no one wanted to buy them. It was extremely disheartening. So we did what seemed like the next logical thing—we made the decision to simply start giving them away. That was in 2000.

"The Worst Cover in the History of Publishing"

One day, in 2005, we saw there was a professional speaker boot camp being held in Las Vegas and decided to go—as always, putting 20 copies of *"Go for No!"* in our suitcase for giveaway purposes.

On the final day of the conference, we still had one book left. We needed someone to give it to. Fortunately, the guy in the row in front of us mentioned he was in sales, so we offered him the final copy, and he took it.

Three days later, we were sitting in the office, and the phone rang. It was the guy we gave the book to. He said:

> *"I'm calling about the book you gave me at the conference in Las Vegas. I want you to know, when I got home, I pulled it out of my bag, glanced at it, and then I threw it in my waste basket."*

And you called to tell us this, *why?*

> *"But the next day,"* he continued, *"when I dumped the stuff in my waste basket in the trash outside, there was your book, right on top. And I thought, 'Okay, I'll read the first page.' An hour later, I'd finished reading the entire book, standing there in the garage next to the trash can. I don't know if you realize it, but I think you've written one of the*

best sales books ever—with the worst cover in the history of publishing! If you're willing to change the cover, I'll take 5,000 copies."

We hung up the phone and said, *"Holy crap! No wonder the mailings didn't work. No one we sent the book to read it because the cover sucks!"*

Time to Get a New Cover

Soon after, we got busy finding a top-notch book cover designer and got the redesign in motion. We also made the decision at that time to formally re-publish the book, adding Andrea's name to the cover as a co-author, which was more than some kind of deceptive marketing tactic.

The truth was, leaving her name off the previous cover was the deception, because she *had* co-written the book. We'd left it off for simplicity, since I (Richard) had been doing the speaking and Andrea had been doing the marketing. Once we decided to hit the road together as co-authors and as a speaking team, the decision was perfectly timed.

NOTE: You're probably wondering what the covers looked like. So, here they are: the original cover *(on the next page)* and the cover re-design that we still use to this day *(on the page after that).*

(original cover)

(cover redesign)

There are two takeaways from this story, just in case you missed them: First, people really *do* judge a book by its cover. And, second, you must have a killer cover, or your cover will kill you. Period.

No, wait—make that *double-period.* .

The Four Levels of Cover Performance

We believe there are "Four Levels of Cover Performance" for any book...

- Level 1...*Your cover sucks.*

- Level 2...*Your cover doesn't suck.*

- Level 3...*Your cover is pretty good.*

- Level 4...*Your cover is great!*

The truth is, it's not easy to create a *great* book cover. Even the big publishing companies occasionally release books with really bad covers. But, at a minimum, you need a *Level 3* cover, one that makes a decent and professional first impression. If your cover is great, well—*that's great.*

But it can't suck.

If your cover sucks, so will your sales because sales require word-of-mouth advertising and good reviews, neither of which will happen if no one reads your book.

Successful Brands Invest Heavily in Product Packaging

Perhaps the biggest difference in the way corporate brands design packaging for their products, as compared to the way authors (and even many cover designers) design book covers is this:

- *One approaches the creation of product packaging as if it was a science, while...*

- *The other approaches product packaging as if it were an art.*

Care to guess which is which?

Corporations create packaging that is carefully designed and tested to do one thing—*to make the product sell*—and they spare no expense in doing so. Many authors, on the other hand, treat the process of cover design as if it were an artistic endeavor.

Big mistake.

Your book cover is not a work of art, even if your book designer thinks it is. It's an advertisement for the product you're selling.

Good (and great) book covers are designed to sell books, not as an artistic outlet for the author and cover designer. As such, the term "cover art" should be forever banned from the publishing industry. Even the term graphic artist is dangerous. What you want is a cover that sells—*and sales is more science than art.*

A Book Cover's First Job Is to "Fit In"

Before we entered the world of writing and book publishing, we would have said, "Of course your cover should be different and stand out from the crowd! You don't want it to look like everyone else's!" This is probably some of the worst thinking we have ever had.

Different is not necessarily better—only different. Your book has a much better chance of being successful if it *fits in* with other covers in the same genre and topic category, *not if it stands out.*

Which reminds us of another story...

> One day I (Richard) was on a trip and having dinner by myself. The restaurant was unique, with a lot of interesting things on the menu—including the wine they served. I ordered a glass of pinot noir, and the waiter said, *"Very good, but I've got to warn you—this wine doesn't come in a bottle, it comes in a can."* In my mind, cans are for soda and beer, right? Now, wine in a can might be convenient for the winery, or the restaurant, but it doesn't comply with a buyer's expectations of how a quality wine is packaged. Then the waiter added, *"But it's really good."*

Well, by this point I was curious, so I took a chance and ordered a can of pinot noir. *(Even writing the words "can of pinot" feels wrong somehow!)*

As it turned out, the waiter was right—the wine was really good. Yet I couldn't help but think about how hard the waiter had to work to sell me on it.

The point is this:

A book cover shouldn't have to work that hard to sell itself. And in the world of Amazon, there won't be anyone standing there explaining why the product packaging (aka, book cover) doesn't seem to fit, telling the reader, *"It's good, trust me!"* Readers will be left to trust their *gut*—and then quickly move on to the next book whose cover meets their preconceived expectations.

None of this means a book's cover needs to be boring, only that it needs to look like it belongs at the party.

Saying you want your cover to be completely different from everyone else's in your book's category/genre is like being in the business of selling oranges and making your oranges a different color. So they'll stand out, you make yours blue. You know what? If you make your oranges blue, they won't sell. Newsflash: *Oranges are orange.* Making your oranges *blue* may get attention, but in the end that attention only confuses people. And confused minds never buy.

Cover Art Should Match the Book's Message

Companies like Proctor & Gamble don't spend millions focusing on overly-artistic packaging. In fact, they go out of their way to use the *least amount of art possible.* And the art they *do* use is usually used to paint a picture of how the buyer will feel once they've purchased and consumed the product.

The problem with most authors is that they tend to lean toward the creative-side of things.

- *They use pictures of sunsets because they think sunsets are beautiful...*

- *They use Mistral font because they think it's interesting, even though no one can read it while browsing tiny thumbnail covers on Amazon...*

- *They use a hot pink background because hot pink was their favorite color when they were a child.*

Interesting and beautiful don't necessarily sell, and if you're smart, your favorite color will be the one that gets people to pull out their credit card and hit the "buy" button.

The "Two-Second" Message Test

Once a book cover has passed the *"I Belong Here"* test, it must then pass the *"Here's What This Book Is About and Why You Should Buy It"* test.

How long does a book have to accomplish this? About three seconds. Maybe less.

The Association for Psychological Science pegs the mind's ability to form a first impression at one-tenth of a second. Being generous, that means your book has no more than two-seconds to communicate what it's about. This, of course, starts with...

Titles & Subtitles: The Hero and the Sidekick

All book titles, whether they're long or short, fit in one of two categories:

1. Self-explanatory titles (titles that tell the reader everything they need to know).

2. Titles that aren't self-explanatory (which is why, on the seventh day, God created subtitles).

For example, some titles that tell you virtually everything you probably need to know to make a buying decision include:

- *"The 7 Habits of Highly Successful People"*
- *"The Success Principles"*
- *"I Will Teach You to be Rich"*
- *"Get Skinny Fast"*
- *"The Happiness Equation"*
- *"Healing Back Pain"*

You read the title and immediately get what the book is about. But more than that, you also get how you will benefit from buying these books and reading them: *Success, Wealth, Thin, Happy and Healthy.*

But Some Titles Need Subtitles to Make Sense

But then there are titles that—without a subtitle—could mean any number of things. For example, consider the following titles where the meaning is either unclear or could be easily misconstrued:

- *The Five-Second Rule*
- *Get the Guy*
- *Take the Stairs*
- *The Four Agreements*

- *Who Moved My Cheese?*

The Five-Second Rule could be about how long you get to inbound a ball in basketball. Or, it could be about how quickly you get to eat a piece of food that has dropped on the floor. It's only when you read the subtitle *("Transform Your Life, Work, and Confidence with Everyday Courage")* that you understand it's a self-help book.

"Get the Guy" could be a book about the mob—or perhaps it's a spy thriller. Then you read the subtitle: *"Learn Secrets of The Male Mind to Find the Man You Want and the Love You Deserve."*

"Take the Stairs" sounds like it might be an exercise book, until you read the subtitle, *"Seven Steps to Achieving True Success,"* that the real meaning becomes clear.

"The Four Agreements" could be a book for lawyers to help create contracts, or a marriage/relationship book—but it's not. The subtitle of *"The Four Agreements"* is: *"A Practical Guide to Personal Freedom."*

And don't get us started about, *"Who Moved My Cheese."*

Virtually All Best-Selling Products Have Subtitles

One of the first things we noticed when doing research on how major corporations design product packaging was how almost every product utilizes a tag line (or *subtitle*) to explain what the product is and what it does.

We studied old ads and packaging for famous products when they were first released, changing how they would be presented if the products were actually books:

Category: *Shave cream*

- Title: *Barbasol®*
- Subtitle: *Means smooth easy sailing through even the toughest beard*

Category: *Detergent*

- Title: *Tide®*
- Subtitle: *Oceans of suds, new washing miracle*

Category: *Cookies*

- Title: *Oreo®*
- Subtitle: *A creamy filled chocolate cookie sandwich*

Category: *Athletic shoes*

- Title: *Converse All-Stars®*
- Subtitle: *America's #1 basketball shoes*

Years later, after the brands were well-established in the mind of the buyer, the tag line/subtitles were no-longer necessary. But initially—when people didn't know what the products were or what they did, they were critical.

Test! Test! Test!

As we mentioned earlier, corporations never release products without doing extensive market research and testing beforehand. And neither should authors.

In our case, we created two potential titles for this book:

1. *"How to Write a Short Book that Will Sell Forever: A Step-by-Step Guide for Self-Published Authors"*

2. *"Million Dollar Book Formula: How to Write a Short Book that Will Sell Forever"*

We went to a website called pickfu.com (a great resource for doing split-tests on just about anything and getting quick feedback) and tested the two titles against each other.

Well, you know the results already, don't you? The second version won, hands down.

One of the other things that's great about PickFu is that the people who vote leave brief comments, which are very valuable when trying to understand *why* people chose one title over another.

The Best Brands Put "Proof" on the Package

Finally, there's this little thing called *proof,* which isn't really little at all.

The best way to think about proof is to imagine that, when someone is looking at a product—detergent, cat food, chocolate, cars, and on and on—they are asking one simple question:

"Who says so besides you?"

Claims and promises made about a product *by the person offering the product* are not proof. They're merely claims. They're promises. *They're advertising.*

"Proof" always comes from an outside third-party. For example, here is a list of statements made on the packaging for a specific brand of butter:

- *New!*
- *2 sticks, net weight 8 oz (226g)*
- *For cooking and baking*
- *Plant steroids to help block cholesterol*
- *28% less saturated fat than butter*
- *11g total fat, 15 mg cholesterol*
- *OMEGA-3s 32mg EPA/DHA, 20% of 160mg DV, 170mg ALA, 10% of 1600mg DV (whatever all that means)*

Wow, that's a lot of content on the front of a fairly small package! But not a word of it is proof. It's all just data and claims.

The same thing is true with books. An author and/or publisher can claim their book is the greatest book ever written, but so what? *You're the author. You're the publisher. What else are you going to say?*

The question is, who says so besides you?

Proof That a Book Is Worth Reading

Offering proof in the world of books comes in the form of the following:

1. *Testimonials (aka, "blurbs" provided by others—the more well-known and respected the better).*

2. *Forewords (having someone else, ideally someone well-known, write a foreword for your book is an implied endorsement).*

3. *Sales rank achieved (for example, "#1 Amazon Bestseller"—for this book and/or other past books you've written).*

4. *Winner (or finalist or semi-finalist in the "Blah Blah" book awards).*

5. *Your credentials as the author (M.D. PhD., MA, etc.).*

Proof won't, in and of itself, make people buy your book if your topic (problem/solution) is of no interest to them. But if they like the title and subtitle, and the book solves a problem for them, the proof you've provided will often serve as the little *push* that nudges them off the fence of indecision to hit the buy button.

The Best Brands Put "Proof" on the Package

Maybe you've seen the clips of Susan Boyle when she appeared as a contestant on the TV program, "Britain's Got Talent," back in the spring of 2009. We sure did. It was one of the most inspiring things we've ever seen, watching Susan step onto that stage—and seeing the look on Simon Cowell's face as he *appraised her package* and made all manner of assumptions, none of which were favorable.

To be fair, Simon's job *was to judge* Susan Boyle—*he was a judge*—but it wasn't fair to judge her by her cover. Or was it?

The truth is, Simon Cowell isn't the only person who *judged Susan Boyle by her cover* that night. We all did. *It's human nature.* It may not be fair, but it is the way it is.

SUCCESS INGREDIENT #6:
PRICING

One of the most important steps for any successful product is to determine how it should be priced.

While there are many pricing strategies to choose from, none of them is guaranteed to work. Even Amazon—as big and as smart and as sophisticated as it is—doesn't know. And that may be why Amazon is constantly adjusting prices on the products it sells, especially when it comes to books.

As associate professor of management science at George Washington University, Charles Toftoy, says: *"Pricing is probably the toughest thing there is to do because it's part-art and part-science."*

Here we go again. *Art and science.*

Get your pricing strategy right, and you can make lots of money with your book. Get your pricing strategy wrong, and you will leave lots of profit on the table.

Major Factors to Consider When Pricing a Book

In our research, looking at how major brands price their products allowed us to identify eight primary factors an author/publisher must consider when pricing a book. Here they are (not in any particular order):

Pricing Factor #1: The Existing Pricing Norms in the Book Market

As a buyer of books yourself, you already know that book prices have basically stagnated over the last decade, a casualty of the digital revolution—coupled with Amazon's stranglehold on the book market. You also know the majority of books fall within a predictable range when it comes to price.

- *Hardcover books (fiction and non-fiction alike) usually fetch between $18-28, assuming we're not talking about college textbooks, in which case, all bets are off*

- *Non-fiction paperbacks usually fall in the $9.99 to $16.99 range*

- *Non-fiction e-books occupy a range usually in the $4.99 to $9.99 range*

- *Then, on the low end, you have fiction e-books, usually priced in the $2.99-4.99 range, unless the author is a big name (in which case the pricing is often higher) or a complete unknown, in which case they may simply make it FREE*

The fact that there are existing price ranges *does not mean* you have no flexibility when it comes to pricing your book. What a book is worth is subjective, at least to some degree. In fact, there is more price elasticity in book pricing than most authors think.

Price elasticity (in case the term is new to you) means the price can be S-T-R-E-T-C-H-E-D like a piece of elastic. Not endlessly, of course—even stretchy elastic has its limits— but it can be stretched more than you think.

Nothing says that, just because other authors price their books cheap, *you* must price your book on the low end to be successful. To the contrary, our research suggests that pricing a book a bit higher than the competition has major advantages.

To understand why, read on.

Pricing Factor #2: The Problem Your Books Solves

The bigger the problem your book solves, the more you can charge...*within limits, of course.* For example, had we priced *"Go for No!"* based on the page count (at only 80 pages), we would have priced it at around $5.95. Instead, we put it out at $12—*double* what we probably should have if we were charging by the page—and for only one reason: *The book solves a significant problem.*

We could make the case that were someone to use the ideas in the book and conquer their fears of failure and rejection, they could land a great job, or start a company, and make a million dollars.

If that's the case, $12 is a bargain.

Remember this: No company is ever just selling a product; it is also selling what that product *does for the buyer*. For example, consider the following two products:

- *Product #1: A typical child's toy/game*

- *Product #2: An emergency "Fire Blanket" (used to smother flames if a fire starts in a kitchen, fireplace, grill, car, camping, etc.)*

The children's game sells for $10. The fire-retardant safety blanket sells for $20, double the price of the game. But here's the thing: The child's game cost the company $2 to produce and package. While the safety blanket cost only .20 cents to produce and package—one-tenth the cost, yet it's double the price.

What it costs to produce something is a non-factor in relation to the perceived value in the eyes of the buyer. Major brands understand this. Many authors forget this.

You are never *just selling a book*—you are also selling what that book *does* for the reader.

- *Books on investing and how to make money can command higher prices than books on getting along with co-workers.*

- *Books that help people eliminate searing back pain can command a higher price than entertainment-oriented fiction.*

- *A book that helps a couple save their marriage can be priced higher than books about helping people to stop biting their nails.*

The bigger the perceived problem being solved, the more you can charge. That's why books should be priced by the problem, not by the cost to produce it or the page count.

Pricing Factor #3: Who You Are Targeting With Your Book

Books targeted at business executives usually support a higher price than books targeted at salespeople, which in turn are generally priced higher than books for the general public. The reasons are obvious. Executives have more money to spend, and greater problems to solve. In the same way, it's a safe bet that salespeople have more money and greater incentive to spend on books than the general public does.

You must consider who your book is targeting and price accordingly. In fact, if you price your book too low (e.g., a book targeted at CEOs with a $9.99 cover price), it will look suspiciously out of place next to other, higher-priced books in the same category.

Pricing Factor #4: Whose Credit Card the Customer Is Paying With

We don't mean *which* credit card someone is using (Visa, MasterCard, American Express), we mean: *Is the buyer paying for the book themselves, or is the company paying?*

If the person is paying with their own funds, they will be more price-sensitive than the business buyer who is charging the book to a company expense account and/or writing the expense off at tax time.

You can always charge more when the buyer is paying with someone else's money.

For example, have you ever noticed how much some office supply stores charge for their office products? It's almost obscene. How do they get away with it? Maybe it has something to do with the fact that most of their customers are company employees—employees who are paying with someone else's money? When someone is paying with someone else's money, price becomes less important.

Pricing Factor #5: The Price Required to Make a Profit

While the upper-end of what can be charged should never be based on a book's page-count, the lower end is totally page-count connected (unless you're selling e-books, of course.)

If you're selling a paperback, you must determine the lowest price you can charge to still make a profit (earn a royalty.)

This does not mean you should charge on the low end of the profit spectrum (please see the factors above) but at least know the price that puts you in the black, not the red.

Pricing Factor #6: If You Are Planning on "Wholesaling" Your Book

If you are planning on wholesaling your book (selling books in quantities at a discount so others can resell them, usually at or near full price), then you must set a cover price that works for all parties.

For example, let's say you publish a 100-page book through Amazon, and you want to buy copies to sell from your website and/or sell through other's websites. The pricing (at the time of this writing) is as follows:

- *A standard 5.5 x 8.5 book (100 pages) would cost you $2.15 per book;*

- *A 150-page book would run $2.65 per book;*

- *A 200-page book would be $3.25 per book;*

- *A 250-page book would be $3.85 per book; and...*

- *A 300-page book would be $4.45 per book.*

Plus, you'll have to pay the shipping charges to get them to you (and the bigger the book, the higher the shipping cost). But here's the most important thing: It doesn't matter if you order one copy, 500 copies or 5,000 copies—the price Amazon charges remains constant. There is no discount to you, as the author, for quantity orders.

This is why you may wish to have a print-run done by an off-set printer. For example, we recently placed an order for 1,000 copies of a 100-page book from our printer in Illinois. The cost to have 1,000 books printed was $1.60 each, plus shipping. Had we purchased the same number of books through Amazon, it would have cost us $2,150 for the same 1,000 copies (35 percent more). And the higher the print-run, the higher the spread. When we order 5,000 copies from our off-set printer, the price comes down to well under $1.00 per book—all of which must be considered when setting the book price.

Pricing Factor #7: The Message You Want to Send About Your Brand

When pricing a book, you also have to consider the message it sends about your brand, and how that message impacts pricing (and profitability) for your other products and services.

For example, imagine two professional speakers each publish books on leadership, which they intend to use to establish themselves as experts on the subject in the marketplace.

- *Author #1 prices his 200-page book at $9.95.*
- *Author #2 prices her 200-page book at $24.00.*

Who do you think has a better chance at getting $10,000 for a one-hour keynote? The answer is obvious.

How you price your book has many considerations that go well beyond the profit made on the book. You must also consider what you want customers to think about you and your business.

This "price higher rather than lower" strategy is especially true if you are using your book to suggest that *you are the best* in any given area. Because if that's the case, offering the cheapest book in your category doesn't make much sense. Don't spend time and money creating the perfect book, with the perfect look, and then sabotage it with an imperfect price strategy.

Pricing Factor #8: The Number of Pages in Your Book

While we started by saying the eight factors were not being presented in any particular order (which they weren't), we *did* place this one last on purpose.

Why? Because most people look at:

- *The problem being solved first*
- *The price of the book second*
- *And the number of pages last*

This is not to say you can ignore page count entirely when pricing your book. As elastic as price may be, you can't triple the price of a 240-page paperback from $12 to $36—you simply can't stretch it that far.

Things You Should Not Consider When Setting Book Prices

Here are three things you should *not* consider when setting your book price:

#1. You should not consider how long it took you to write your book.

If writing time were a factor, then all books that took 10 years to write would be the highest priced, which is ridiculous. Just because it took you five years to finish your book, that's no reason the buyer should pay more for it.

#2. You should not consider how much money you spent on editing, a cover, website, etc.

Again, this is not the buyer's problem. Just because a company spent $25 million developing a vacuum cleaner, that doesn't mean they can charge you $30,000 to buy one.

#3. You should not consider the fact that you have a co-author (or multiple co-authors) with whom you need to split the royalties.

Again, this is not the buyer's problem. Two or three authors does not double or triple the value of the book to the reader.

SUCCESS INGREDIENT #7:
PLACEMENT

Placement is where a company *places* its products so it can be found by the prospects for whom they are intended. In the grocery business, this usually means on store shelves. For clothing manufacturers, it means hanging on racks in retail stores at the mall. And for authors and publishers, it once meant getting their books on shelves in bookstores. Then the internet changed everything.

Enter Amazon.

Today, half of all books sold worldwide are sold through Amazon. Authors can place their book in one location (on a single platform) and have access to 50 percent of the marketplace, which is great.

However, Amazon's enormous power and reach has given it a *stranglehold leverage* over authors and publishers. This means it can change the rules regarding how products are sold on its platform anytime it wants.

Which Amazon often does.

Some authors have started to push back, looking for ways to navigate the book marketing universe without Amazon. And it's not that authors *can't* make it without Amazon—many do. But there is a reason to make Amazon *the* place to focus your book marketing efforts, and that is:

> *When the market is dominated by one big dog—the big dog in this case being Amazon—you want to get along with that dog. In fact, you don't just want to get along with the big dog...you want the big dog to love you.*

When you focus your marketing efforts on Amazon, and your sales reach a certain level, Amazon's algorithm kicks in and shows you love by promoting your book within the platform.

All Sales Forced onto a Single Platform

This is a reason we've been able to keep *"Go for No!"* among the top bestsellers of our chosen sub-lists for over 10-years. If we had spread our sales over multiple platforms, we probably would not have ranked on any of them. Splitting your marketing efforts by placing your book everywhere dilutes the total number of books you sell on *any one* platform. How? It:

1. *Makes it harder to hit Amazon's bestseller lists, which...*

2. *Reduces the chances of Amazon's algorithm kicking in to market your book to other shoppers.*

In short, Amazon rewards loyalty. The more books an author sells on its platform, the happier Amazon is. The happier Amazon is, the more it promotes the author's book on its site.

Placement Is <u>Not</u> Promotion

Now, you might see some publishers and distributors that will tout getting your book (and/or e-book) into dozens or more online book stores. And don't get us wrong, there are a lot of wonderful places out there where people can buy books, so it's great to be there. No harm, no foul. Maybe a person here and there will stumble across your book. Good. But don't be lulled into thinking that simply having your book on a shelf will move books. It won't.

Because placement is not a substitute for promotion.

And yet, sadly, we've spoken to many authors who believed that simply having their book available in every possible nook and cranny of the book-buying universe was going to help sales.

Remember this: Placement does not equal promotion or sales. To make "placement" pay off, you need to use your own proactive marketing efforts to drive people to all those various locations. But then, to what end?

And that leads us to the next ingredient...

SUCCESS INGREDIENT #8:
PROMOTION

In the old days, marketing your book meant you had to buy ads in newspapers and magazines, get reviewed in trade publications, and mail or fax press releases to media outlets. These days, it's mostly about marketing online. Which is great, of course, because you can conduct 90 percent of your promotional efforts on your phone or laptop while sitting at your local Starbucks.

But just because book marketing is convenient, doesn't mean it's easy. The marketplace is crowded and competitive.

Think of it this way: A brand gets its new soup on the shelf at your local supermarket. But the mere act of *placement,* even with excellent packaging, does not guarantee success. It still needs promotion.

Sadly, some authors think all they have to do is upload their book file, and Amazon is going to make their book a best seller. This is simply not the case.

This is not to say that Amazon won't help market and promote your book. Oh, they will—eventually—but only *after* you've driven enough traffic to your book and sold enough copies to prove there is a demand for what you've produced. Then, and only then, does Amazon (or any other bookseller) become interested in recommending your book to its customers.

But what if I get a traditional publishing deal? Certainly the publisher will market the book?

Nope. Sorry.

Once you're a well-known author (with a name like Grisham, Godin or Gladwell), then, yes, you'll get marketing support for your book. Lots of it. But not until then. It's only after a book starts to sell that other people get interested in promoting it. Once the snowball starts rolling down the hill, others will jump on for the ride. Until then, you're on your own.

We're not telling you this to get you depressed, only to splash a bit of cold water in your face to the reality of the situation. If you write a book—with or without a traditional publisher—*there's work to be done.*

It's not Amazon's job to make your book a best seller. It's your job. Nor is it the job of publisher—unless you *are* the publisher, in which case, it is very much your job still.

Case Study: The "Chicken Soup for the Soul®" Story

With over 500-million copies sold, Mark Victor Hansen and Jack Canfield's *"Chicken Soup for the Soul®"* book series is, perhaps, the greatest success story in the history of publishing.

Few people know the whole story, however.

After Mark & Jack got their book deal, they purchased a copy of John Kremer's *"1001 Ways to Market Your Book"* and committed to implementing five ideas from the book every day. Five things. Every single day.

Whether it was giving a talk at a public library, going on a radio show, sending a free copy of *Chicken Soup* to a book reviewer, or writing an article for a newsletter—it didn't matter. They did five promotional activities a day, every day, for several years.

Though Mark and Jack knew they had a special book on their hands, they knew something even more important. They knew that the book would not sell without promotion, and they knew the promotion was *their* job, *not* the publisher's.

The rest, as they say, is history.

The Best Ways to Promote Your Book

There are at least 100 different things you *could* do to promote your book, but without knowing what your book is about and who your target prospects are, it's impossible to say precisely which strategies would be best for *you* and *your* book. Filling the next 10 pages with a laundry list of possible ways you *could* promote your book is not a good use of space or of time—after all, all you need to do is Google *"How to Market and Promote Books,"* and the answers are all right there.

We think the best thing we can offer is to do a *deep dive* into the *one universal strategy* all authors should have at the center of their marketing and promotional efforts.

The Promotional Strategy of "Influencing the Influencers"

The concept of promoting products and services through influencers (also known as *Influencer Marketing*) is not new. Yet, its amazing how many authors do not use it effectively...or ignore it entirely.

So, what is an influencer? An influencer is someone who:

- *Others look to for their opinion*
- *Inspires large groups of people because of their following/platform*
- *Already has the trust and respect of others*

Because of the above, they exert a certain amount of influence, including purchasing decisions. And they don't have to be a Kardashian to be influential. They need only be someone with an audience that aligns with the prospects for your book, such as:

- *Bloggers/columnists*
- *Radio talk show hosts/Podcasters*
- *Other authors/professional speakers*
- *Business owners/association leaders*
- *"Celebrities" (large and small)*

And the list goes on and on.

The best promotional marketing strategy you can employ is always to work "top down" by focusing your attention on key critical influencers with an audience that aligns with your target reader.

KEY INFLUENCER

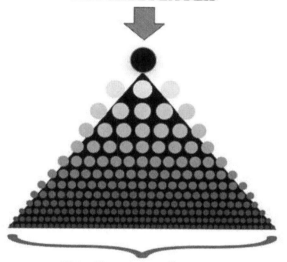

The target audience you want to reach

MillionDollarBookFormula.com

Daymond John Finds an Influencer for FUBU

Most people know Daymond John from his involvement on the hit show, "Shark Tank," sitting alongside Dallas Maverick's owner Mark Cuban and New York real estate icon, Barbara Corcoran. What most people don't know is the story of how he got there.

John started his career in fashion in the 1980s, making and selling wool hats under the brand name FUBU (which stood for "For Us, By Us"). During his off hours, John would visit music video sets and ask rappers to wear various FUBU apparel in the shoot. Several rappers did, and the brand began to get traction. The big break came when LL Cool J decided to wear FUBU on a video with the group Boyz II Men.

As John says, "Our product was front and center on the biggest and most influential personalities for our core consumers."

That, in a nutshell, is influencer marketing.

Reviewers Are Influencers, Too

According to research done by Nielsen, here is the order in which people rank trust:

1. *Recommendations from people they know*

2. *Consumer reviews/opinions posted online*

3. *Editorial content on TV and in newspapers*

4. *Ads on TV*

5. *Ads in newspapers/magazines*

6. *Ads on radio*

7. *Billboards/other outdoor advertising*

8. *Emails people signed up for*

9. *Online video advertising*

10. *Ads on social media*

11. *Online banner ads*

12. *Text ads on mobile phones*

While the #1 item on the list goes to prove our point, it's important not to gloss-over the fact that the #2 item on the list is *consumer reviews and opinions posted online*. Surveys point to the fact 92 percent of consumers read online reviews and trust recommendations posted online by *strangers* as much as they do from friends (assumedly because there's not perceived *profit motive* attached to the opinion being offered). This is one of the reasons book reviews matter so much—*because book reviewers are influencers in their own right*. Any one reviewer may not have a large following, but this person's reviews— collectively—carry enormous influence with potential buyers.

Quantity and Quality Both Matter

This is why it is critical for an author to get at least 25 reviews as fast as possible (and ideally 100+ reviews), since a mere ponderance of reviews suggests readership, which is an implied recommendation all on its own. For example, what does it say to you when you see a book that's been out for 14 months and has zero reviews?

Point made.

That said, in your haste to reach the above-mentioned numbers, be careful not to run afoul of Amazon's review guidelines. In particular:

- *Don't have people connected to you give a review for your book.*

- *Don't exchange reviews with other authors, review for review. If you do, Amazon will pull the review—and if they think you've really abused the review system, they could pull your book altogether.*

- *Don't pay or incentivize anyone for a review.*

You can give a copy of your book to someone to review, but this person needs to disclose *in their review* that they were given the book in exchange for an honest review.

Now that we've scared you silly, how to do you get reviews? Simple. You get them the same way Daymond John got influential rappers to wear his FUBU brand.

He asked.

Ask, Ask, Ask. Then Ask Some More.

You must:

- *Ask for reviews on your social media channels...*

- *Ask for them in your newsletter if you have one...*

- *Ask readers to leave a review at the end of your book...*
- *Ask anyone who calls or sends an email providing you positive feedback if they'd be kind enough to post it...*

And when people tell you they will write a review, but then don't, you need to ask again.

The reality is, many authors shy away from asking for reviews. They assume if someone loves the book, that person will go review it on their own. Most people won't—*unless you ask them to.*

Is getting reviews a lot of work, especially in the beginning? Yes. Did we mention yet how promotion is your job?

Influencer Marketing Is Not a One-Time Thing

To be sure, influencer marketing is not a strategy you try once, just to see what happens. It is an ongoing, never-ending process of identifying key influencers and doing what it takes to connect with them.

In our case, nearly two decades after we released *"Go for No!"*, we continue to gift copies of *"Go for No!"* to people who would appreciate it and could be influential for us. It might be a podcaster, a fellow author, a vice-president of sales at a major corporation, a professional speaker who trains salespeople, and on and on.

We didn't sell 400,000 copies of our book by accident. We worked hard, but we also worked *smart*—and making the *influencer strategy* the core of our marketing efforts was the smartest thing we ever did.

SUCCESS INGREDIENT #9:
PLATFORM

According to Writer's Digest magazine, an author platform is "your **visibility** as an author." Then there's a great definition provided by publishing expert Jane Friedman, who defines a platform as "an ability to sell books because of who you are or who you can **reach**."

Regardless of which definition you prefer, the two most important words contained in them are:

VISIBILITY and REACH.

For example, being a regular on radio or television (or even having a popular podcast) gives you, as an author, visibility and reach. People know who you are. And, if you write a book, you can tell your following about it, and where and when to get it. You see TV personalities doing this all the time.

Now, we've heard some authors say, "Amazon is my platform."

Let's get something straight:

> Amazon is *a* platform. But it's not *your* platform.
> It's *Amazon's* platform. You're just a guest.

Why do we say this?

As big of fans as we are of Amazon as a platform, it's important to understand that your visibility and reach there is not owned by you—*Amazon owns it.* It's as if you were invited to speak at a conference to a group of employees. Being invited to speak there does not make it your company.

You are a guest there.

In the same way, your visibility and reach on Amazon is on loan, and that visibility can go away at the snap of Amazon's fingers. And it's the same with Barnes & Noble and Kobo and with every other book selling platform.

Here is one of the most important things we are going to say in this entire book, so we're going to put it in bold, 14-point Impact font...

If you want to build a business, not just sell books, you <u>must</u> build a platform that you own and control.

What we're saying is: Every marketing activity you engage in on OPP (Other People's Platforms) must include a strategy that drives those people to YP (Your Platform).

So, as we move forward in this section, please notice that every suggestion we make—even if it includes using other people's platforms—drives people to you so you can build your platform.

Which Comes First, Your Book or Your Platform?

Before we dig into recommended actions for building a great author platform, let's address the question: *Do you need to have an established platform before writing your book?*

The answer is, *no.*

Nothing says you must have an established platform before you write and launch your book, but the chances of being successful right out of the gate without a platform are much smaller. We don't say this to be discouraging, we say it to be honest.

That said, just because you don't have a platform, doesn't mean you shouldn't write a book. Writing a book is one of the best ways to build a platform.

For example, we did not have anything even remotely resembling a platform when we wrote our very first book, *Retail Magic,* which we used primarily as a marketing tool to sell speaking engagements. The same thing was true when we wrote *"Go for No!",* and we were very successful with this as our approach—but here's what we did wrong. We didn't go out of our way to build an email list of the people who had been in the audience when we spoke. *It never even crossed our minds.*

Your Email List Is the Centerpiece of Your Platform

There is no doubt that an email list is the most important part of an author's platform. *We know that now.*

Sadly for us, eight years after we'd launched our business, our email list had less than 300 names on it—even though we'd spoken to tens of thousands of people. We weren't aware enough to realize, while we were making money and doing well in the present, we weren't doing anything to build our platform for the future.

Learn from our mistake. You should be working on building your platform from the earliest moment you can.

Your email list is without a doubt the most powerful sales and marketing tool you can possess—"possess" being a key term here, because it indicates ownership. Your email list is something you build and own. In fact, ask virtually any business guru if they had to lose everything in their business except one thing, what would it be? Ninety-nine percent of them will say their email list. Why? Because it is that valuable.

Don't Just Build a List, Build Relationships

You may have heard the saying: *The money is in the list.* The first time we heard it was from marketing guru, Dan Kennedy. A lot of people take credit for having said it first, and whether it was Dan or someone else, it's true—*well, mostly true.* The money isn't really *in* the list—it's in the relationship you have with the people on the list. Because it's the relationship that makes the list responsive to whatever it is you have to offer, be it another book or an online course, etc.

In our case, we adopted the newsletter strategy back in 2007 (once we got smart enough to start growing our list), which has allowed us to establish ongoing communication with the people on our list. It's not that a newsletter is the only (or best) way to go, but it has worked very well for us in our business.

Your Website

Let's start by saying you can definitely sell books without having a website, but it's almost impossible to be successful without one. Besides, you need a place where people can come to sign-up for your email. Logically, that place is your website.

Your website doesn't have to be large or complicated. In fact, a simple website can be even more effective than an expensive, lots-of-bells-and-whistles site. The most common elements include:

- A simple and easy-to-navigate Home Page.

- An "About You" page (containing your bio, picture).

- A "Follow Us" section (with your various social media links).

- An "About Your Book" page (which might be the main content on your Home Page).

- A Blog (if you have/want one).

- And, most important of all, an "Email Sign Up" section (or pop-up box).

That's it.

Eventually—when time and money allow for it—you might want a more elaborate website. But for the purposes of building your platform, that's all you need.

Using Social Media to Build Your Platform

As important as social media can be to your business, your email list will have a far greater impact on sales over time. How much more impact are we talking about? We use *The Rule of 10* as a guide, which suggests that for every name on your email list, you'll need 10-times as many social media followers to sell the same number of books. And with the way things are going, it might become The Rule of 20.

Does this mean social media doesn't work for book marketing? No, it does. Just don't think that you will get the same bang for your buck from a social media post as you will from sending an email to your list. Why? For one simple reason:

People who follow you on social media have displayed a mild interest in you and/or your content, while people who took the time to visit your website/landing page and have opted-in to your mailing list have displayed a greater level of interest (10-times greater, probably.)

And, at the risk of sounding like we're beating a dead horse—the following you *do* establish is yours only as long as the platform you build that following on allows you to have it.

Your Twitter following belongs to Twitter. It's their platform. They own it, not you. You're merely a guest at their party. And it's the same with Facebook. And

Instagram. And Snapchat. And YouTube. And every other platform you may be building on.

None of this is to suggest you shouldn't be using these platforms to build yours. It's only to remind you that your goal when using OPPs is to be looking for clever and effective ways to drive their followers to *your* website.

Using Public Speaking to Build Your Platform

Because our books were designed to get speaking engagements, we thought of the speech as the end of the process. That was a mistake. What an opportunity we missed by not giving people in the audience a compelling reason to visit our website (a free report, for example) where we'd have the opportunity to capture their contact information and get them on our list.

Today, when we speak, we offer audience members a free *NO-Quotient*™ assessment that measures and scores their fear of rejection. Not everyone comes, but many have— enough that we've built our email list from 300 people to almost 20,000.

By the way, nothing says you have to be paid to use this list-building technique. In fact, using this method to build your platform turns every speech into a speech you will get paid something for down the road as you market to the list you've built.

Building a Platform Through Podcasts

While we have never launched a podcast of our own, we have used other people's podcasts, by going on as their guest—not only to promote our books and speaking, but also to drive *their* audience to our website to build *our* platform. How? In the same way we drive people in the audience at speaking engagements to our list by offering a free gift.

Hopefully you're seeing the pattern here. Whether you're posting a video on YouTube, tweeting, giving a talk at IBM or the Rotary club, being interviewed on someone's podcast or radio/TV show—*you are crashing their platform*. And every moment you are doing so, you should be looking for ways to make the people on *their* platform part of *your* platform.

Big Companies Have Been Slow to Act

As we studied how big brands built their businesses, it was interesting to see how many of them made the same mistake of marketing through other's platforms, while completely ignoring their own.

- *Brands selling products through supermarkets were always at the mercy of the supermarket chain (which owned the sales platform) making the decision to cut them off and no longer carry their product—leaving the brand with no way of communicating with the customers they've lost...*

- *Music labels sold their product through record stores, only to find themselves with no platform of their own when the Internet exploded...*

- *And book publishers spent a hundred years placing author's books on bookstore shelves, not realizing they weren't building their own platform-based connection with the buyers of those books—only to discover themselves empty-handed when those same bookstores went out of business.*

In fairness, the case could be made that the above examples were all victims of the digital age—that they had no way of seeing it coming. Perhaps. But even after the handwriting was on the wall, they were all slow to act.

Some of them still aren't acting.

SUCCESS INGREDIENT #10:
PARTNERING

The idea of two or more people partnering with each other to grow or build an entire business is nothing new:

- *English candle maker, William Procter, and Irish soap maker, James Gamble, partnered to create one of the most successful companies in the world.*

- *Jenn Hyman and Jenny Fleiss, who started with nothing but an idea yet brought their own expertise to launch a subscription-based service renting fashionable clothing (called "Rent the Runway") valued today at $800 million.*

- *Henry Wells and William Fargo, Ben Cohen and Jerry Greenfield, Bill Hewlett and Dave Packard, Oprah Winfrey and Gayle King, Orville and Wilber Wright, and let's not forget "The Steves" (as in Jobs & Wozniak).*

Oprah Winfrey and Gayle King's partnership is particularly interesting.

While Oprah's meteoric rise to fame and fortune has gained her worldwide recognition, with a net worth in excess of $3 billion, there has always been one person by her side—her longtime friend Gayle King—whom Oprah met working at a Baltimore TV station in 1976.

Would Oprah have made it on her *own* (pun intended)? Who knows. What we do know is that the partnership between the two women significantly accelerated that success.

Does This Mean You Must Partner With Others?

Are we suggesting that to be successful that you, as an author, must partner with someone else to achieve success? Yes, we are.

No one does it alone.

For example: When we launched *Success in 100 Pages* (our new publishing imprint), we, in effect, entered into a partnership with authors Ray and Jessica Higdon, wherein:

- *They, as authors, brought their knowledge, expertise and platform to the party.*

- *We brought our knowledge, expertise, and publishing services.*

When you think about it this way, every author/publisher arrangement in the world is a partnership to some degree.

This is not to suggest that you must be "published" by a publishing company to be successful. But we did look for ways to partner with other authors. Without these many partnerships, our book would never have been a success.

Partnering Through Cross-Promotion

Cross promotion is typically where you and another party agree to share your work with each other's platforms. In other words, a promotional trade.

One such cross-promotional activity is a simple newsletter article swap. In the online world today, we call it *guest blogging*. Even if only one party is contributing an article for a newsletter or blog, each party is benefiting from the arrangement:

- *The author benefits by getting exposure to the other person's following/platform.*

- *The person with the platform benefits by being able to provide fresh content to his/her following without having to produce it.*

Partnering by Co-Authoring a Book

The next form of partnering, one you see done all the time, is co-authoring.

You don't see co-authoring a lot in the fiction world, usually because creatives tend to protect their artistic choices to the death and having to battle with a co-author can be problematic.

However, in the non-fiction world—where people are not building worlds of fantasy and developing characters but sharing expertise on a subject—co-authoring is quite common, and there are a lot of positive reasons for doing so.

The benefits to having a co-author include:

- *Getting your book out faster if you each take sections to write.*

- *Sharing in the cost of the book's editing, production and marketing.*

- *Each co-author brings knowledge and expertise the other does not possess.*

In most cases, each author shares equally in the costs, and each author shares in the net proceeds after the book is sold. In some instances, however, one author may command a greater, *unequal* share of the profit because they do more of the writing and/or due to the size and reach of that author's platform.

All of this is negotiable, of course.

For example, an unknown author who does most of the writing might be paired-up with a famous, well-known author (or celebrity) to co-author a book. When this happens, chances are good the profit spilt is *not* 50/50. The split might be 60/40 or even 80/20.

Any guess as to who gets the bigger share?

The most important thing is that you, as a co-author, get what you want from the arrangement. You might co-author with someone strictly for the money, but you might also want to co-author to learn from that person, put yourself on the map credibility-wise, or simply to build a relationship that you wouldn't have access to otherwise— even if the profit split is not in your favor.

The Chicken & Egg Problem in Partnering

The biggest challenge when trying to partner is that others usually want to partner with people who have existing platforms. This is why the platform ingredient comes before the partnering ingredient.

The important thing to know is that the size of your platform does not need to be equal in size to get others interested in partnering with you. Someone with a 100,000-person email list or subscriber base still wants to get his or her book and/or other products in front of a 10,000-person list if your list represents a new prospect base for them.

Becoming Business Partners...For Real

Finally, there's the possibility of actually becoming someone's true business partner. While this is obviously not something you need to worry about, especially if you're first starting out, relationships do evolve.

Our non-legal advice is, be careful. Partnerships are famous for going south. We'd rather see you famous for your book, not for your appearance on Judge Judy.

SUCCESS INGREDIENT #11:
PROGRESSION

First, what do we mean by progression?

For some people, finishing their book is the end of their writing career—they set out with the goal to write one book, and now they have. That's it, the end of the road. For others the book they've written is only the beginning.

Tide® was Proctor & Gamble's first product in the detergent category, but the product line didn't stop there: it *progressed* into a complete line with a wide assortment of additional products.

For authors, a book is a single source of income from which multiple sources of income may grow. It's a tree on which there are many branches. After all, you did all the work writing the book. Why stop there?

The point we want to stress here is that even if you don't make a million dollars directly from the sales of your book, you could very well bring in a million dollars here, through the process of *progression*.

Many Ways to Monetize Your Knowledge

Though there are countless ways of monetizing knowledge gained in the process of researching and writing your book, we're going to focus on the six most well-known and profitable categories (again, not in any particular order).

Category #1: Audio Books

The age of audio is upon us, with audio books proving to be the fastest growing format today. According to the Pew Research Center, audiobook listeners have increased 14 percent in just the past year, a trend driven by busy lifestyles, mobile devices, and the abundance of high-quality programming that is now available. In fact, it's virtually impossible to find a mainstream book for which there isn't an audio version available.

For this reason, we believe you must have an audio version of your book if you're serious about reaching your target audience.

Category #2: More Books

Quite often, this takes the form of a book series. Some of our favorite examples include:

- The *"Miracle Morning"* series, by Hal Elrod
- Bob Burg and John David Mann's *"Go Giver"* series
- The *"Savvy Way"* book series, by Gundi Gabriel

And there are many, many others.

It's also good to know that if you do well with your first book, Amazon will be even more inclined to pay attention when you release something new; in particular, something that may be of interest to the readers who bought your previous book.

Category #3: Products, Courses and Webinars

If your topic lends itself to more detailed, behind-the-scenes information beyond what is contained in your book, you can develop a course that will generate 100-times the income you can earn with a book alone.

When we started our business, CDs and DVDs had just overtaken the cassette tape industry. Today, everything is going online, which is wonderful for authors.

Advances in technology have made it incredibly easy to share information with people anywhere in the world, which has changed the way humans learn and consume knowledge. It has also made the barrier to entry remarkably low for producers of such content, especially when you consider the low production costs, no storage and zero shipping.

Category #4: Speaking, Training, Coaching & Consulting

We've already talked quite a bit about paid speaking in this book, but that's because of the enormous back-end income speaking provides. Suffice it to say, many a professional speaking career has been launched through the writing of a book—from Zig Ziglar to Jan Sincero, and from Tony Robbins to Mel Robbins.

And then there's training. If your topic lends itself to more formal, in-depth training, there is significant money to be earned in this already-established and lucrative area. Plus, there's coaching, a field that has taken off over the last 20 years—both in the area of business and life coaching.

Category #5: Live Events

Just because online learning is growing by leaps and bounds doesn't mean live, in-person events are going away. To the contrary, seminars and live events are thriving.

Does the message of your book lend itself to a live event? It probably does.

Category #6: Membership Sites and Mastermind Groups

A membership site is fundamentally a website where you pay to belong. Like being a member of a gym, you pay a monthly fee to get access to special content, ongoing training or coaching—whatever the creator of the membership site wants to provide.

For a new author, developing a membership site may feel pretty advanced, but we share it to keep you thinking about what is eventually possible because of your book.

Then there are mastermind groups.

If membership sites are a product of the Internet age, mastermind groups go back at least 100 years. The term "mastermind" and was coined in 1925 by author Napoleon Hill in his book *"The Law of Success"* and used again later in *"Think and Grow Rich."*

A mastermind is a relatively small group of people who support, challenge and collaborate with one another—usually in an area of focused interest, like success...or wealth-building...or solving homelessness...or perhaps book marketing?

And Anything Else You Can Imagine

Seriously, there are so many ways to progress from a book that we'd need an entire book to cover them all *(oh, the irony)*.

It's important to understand we are not saying you should do all these things—in fact, we'll go so far as to say you shouldn't, any more than you should order everything on the menu at a restaurant. This is merely a menu of possibilities, to expand your thinking.

SUCCESS INGREDIENT #12:
PROTECTION

The more we looked at how major brands created and marketed products, the more we noticed how many times we came across instructions, disclaimers, product warnings, and symbols (including but not limited to) ™ ® ©, and many others. In other words, there was a lot of butt-covering going on.

Authors often fall down in this area.

Speaking of butt-covering:

Disclaimer: *We are not lawyers, and we don't pretend to be. As such, nothing presented on the following pages is intended as legal advice (for that matter, nothing in this entire book is intended to be.)*

That said, here are six things you absolutely must be aware of:

1. Copyright your material.

The good news is, the moment you create content, you own the copyright for that material—whether you register it, publish it, add the little © symbol, or not. This does not mean there aren't other things you should do to protect your work—including registering the work with the United States Copyright Office.

As an FYI, your copyright lasts from the moment your work first appears in tangible form until 70 years after your death. This was _not_ always the case.

Also, the copyright for a work prepared by two or more co-authors lasts for 70 years after the last surviving author's death.

2. Establish a legal business entity.

Whether you should incorporate your business as an "S-Corp," LLC or other legal entity, that's up to you (based on advice from a qualified legal source). In our case, we operate under an "S-Corp" for both legal protection and for tax advantage purposes—which does not mean you should—nor is doing so a requirement for you to publish a book. But there are sound reasons for doing so, and you should be aware of your options.

3. Choose a name for your publishing company.

The name of our company and our publishing company are the same. For simplicity, you may want to do the same thing and use a single name for both...or not...depending on how complex your business is and how you want it structured.

4. Check your title for established trademarks.

Unless you are establishing a series of two or more books with the same title—for example, a series like *"Chicken Soup for the Soul"*—book titles can't be trademarked. This means you can go out and write a book called *"Gone with the Wind"* if you want to. But why would you? There are just too many opportunities for creativity to follow in someone else's footsteps.

Also, check to see if anyone has an established trademark for the name of your book. This is especially important if you're attempting to build a brand, as we did when we chose *"Go for No!"* as our book title. It makes no sense to write a book and invest in marketing, only to find out the name is trademark-protected.

This is done by doing a search at the United States Patent and Trademark Office website at: www.USPTO.gov. You may also need to do additional local searches in your state.

5. ISBN numbers.

ISBN is short for *International Standard Book Number*, which is a thirteen-digit identifier that goes on the copyright page of your book. ISBNs are purchased from R. R. Bowker, which is the U.S. agency licensed to sell them.

You'll need to purchase a different ISBN for each different version or format your book will be published in. This means if you are going to publish a hardcover version of your book, a paperback version, a Kindle version and an audio version, you'll need four different ISBNs, one for each. Plus, if you're doing different language versions of your book—Spanish, for example—you'll need a separate ISBN for that, as well.

And no, they are not cheap.

- A single ISBN is $125.

- A block of 10 ISBNs costs $295 (making the price $29.50 each).

- A block of 100 ISBNs is $575 (dropping the cost to only $5.75 per/ISBN).

It doesn't take a rocket scientist to see that if you're going to publish a book and need an ISBN for each of the three most common formats (paperback, e-book and audio), you'll want to jump in and start with a block of ten.

6. Register domain names

It's also important to register any and all domain names you may want or need, especially if you are using your book to establish a brand. In our case, since *"Go for No!"* is our book title *and* our brand, it was imperative we owned goforno.com. We also own go4no.com (in case someone types it in that way) as well as gofortheno.com (because we heard people accidently say it that way), each of which is directed to the same website.

Owning various versions also ensures that our competition won't buy these domains and end up with traffic that *we* generated with *our* marketing being directed to *their* website.

The above is <u>not</u> a complete list

The six items outlined above is by no means designed to serve as a complete list of legal considerations when publishing a book. Things like Errors & Omissions insurance, the writing of formal legal disclaimers, the use of photos and quotes in a book—all of these need to be considered. If you can afford to consult with an attorney, you should. And if you can't afford one, at a bare minimum, you must follow the guidelines in the following three books:

- *"The Self-Publisher's Legal Handbook,"* by Helen Sedwick

- *"Business and Legal Forms for Authors and Publishers,"* by Tad Crawford

- *"The Fine Print of Self-Publishing,"* by Mark Levine

Collectively, all three books will cost you under $50. Over time, they'll be worth 1,000 times that.

SUCCESS INGREDIENT #13:
PERSISTENCE

Most book marketing these days looks like this: A big book launch, a rapid sharp spike in sales, followed by an equally rapid fall back to the Earth.

We think this approach is a mistake.

So does *Proctor & Gamble®, Ford®, Nike®, Coca-Cola®,* and every other successful brand in the world. Because no brand launches a product with the intent of letting it crash back to Earth. The intent of the launch is to get the product outside of Earth's gravity where it can stay for a long, long time.

That takes planning and persistence.

For example, *"Go for No!"* has an average Amazon Sales Rank of 4,593 over the last eight-years. This was achieved because we supported the book with consistent marketing. In fact, we didn't even do a launch. It never crossed our minds.

What we've proven with *"Go for No!"* is that, in the end, the tortoise absolutely *will* eventually beat the hare. Just because a book doesn't *fly off the shelves* during its launch period, that doesn't mean the book is bad or that the game is over. Good books take time to find an audience. Slow and steady wins the race.

Why Your Book Should Be "Evergreen"

Having a long-term book-marketing mentality assumes the content is "evergreen" in nature—something that isn't going to become dated and obsolete in just a year or two.

If the content in your book is evergreen, it doesn't get old. It never dies. It sells forever.

For example, two of the best-selling books of all time in the personal development genre—*"Think and Grow Rich"* and *"How to Win Friends and Influence People"* are evergreen because they are based on timeless philosophies. Even though much of language is dated, readers give it a pass because it's the lessons they care about—lessons that were effective when they were first written and will still be effective 100 years from now.

If you write a book about investing in Bitcoin, it may do well because Bitcoin is a hot topic at the time of this writing. *(Note: If you're reading this book in the year 2038 and don't know what Bitcoin is, we've just made our point about evergreen content—that, and a lot of people lost a ton of money.)*

When Your Book Simply Isn't Selling

So, what if you've written a book and it simply isn't selling? How do you know when it's time to throw in the towel?

Admittedly, if your book isn't selling, you have a problem. The question is: *What kind of problem do you have?*

- *Maybe you have a **"problem"** problem.*

What we mean is: *Does your book really solve a problem?* If it does, great. Then...

- *Maybe you have a **"prospect"** problem.*

Even if your book solves a problem, is it a problem people know they have? One they are actively searching for a solution to? If not, you might be in trouble. But if there are prospects for your book, then...

- *Maybe you have a **"product"** problem.*

In other words, is the content of your book compelling enough that the people who read it want to tell others about it, providing you the word-of-mouth necessary to drive sales? If you're satisfied that your content is buttoned-up, then...

- *Maybe you have a **"packaging"** problem.*

Is the title attention-getting? Does the subtitle make it clear who the book is for and make a promise? Have you created a killer cover? If you can answer yes, then...

- *Maybe you have a **"pricing"** problem.*

Is the price for your book too high? Too low? If you're convinced that your book is priced properly and it's still not selling...

- *Maybe you a have a **"placement"** problem.*

Maybe your book is in the wrong place. Or places. Or in too few places. Or perhaps it's in too many places. Test. Try different platforms. Maybe driving people to *your* website will work better for your book? Or...

- *Maybe you have a **"promotion"** problem.*

More accurately, maybe you have a lack of promotion problem. Are you simply waiting for people to stumble across your book? Are you proactively engaged in actions that drive traffic to your book? If you are, then...

- *Maybe you have a **"platform"** and/or **"partnering"** problem.*

Have you taken the steps necessary to build your platform? Have you worked to influence the influencers in your topic area? Are you developing relationships with people who already have established platforms? If the answer is yes...

- *Maybe you simply haven't given your book enough time to find an audience.*

Yes, maybe you have a **persistence** problem.

Without trying to sound cliché, you've got to be willing to try and fail...and try and fail again...*and again*...until you finally achieve what you set out to do.

Everyone sees the success of bestselling books, and they think it's easy. Yes, it can be. Overnight successes do happen. But we need to say this as clearly and directly as we can:

Overnight success is extremely rare.

And this brings us back to where we started this program, with the first of the 13 Success Ingredients...

Purpose.

When the going gets tough, remind yourself why you wrote your book in the first place. *What was your purpose?* Was it simply to make money? Was it to help people solve a problem? Did you want to change the world?

The world doesn't get changed by people who quit.

Your book is your baby—don't abandon it just because it isn't living up to your expectations as quickly as you hoped. Love it. Nurture it. Raise it until it becomes what it is destined to be.

Trust us—no one is going to fight for your book like you will. And no one will ever care more about your book than you.

We wrote *"Go for No!"* in December 1999. We published for the first time in January 2000. It finally hit #1 on the Amazon Sales & Selling list on December 31, 2010...*11 years later.*

So, here's the question: *When, exactly, should we have given up on our book?* After the first mailing bombed? At year two? Year five? We shudder to think about what our lives would have been like if we had decided to simply throw in the towel.

Making your book a success is not easy. Plan on having to fight to get your book seen, purchased and read. And that means committing to being in it for the long haul.

After you publish your book, when you find yourself feeling like giving up, remember we said all this. And then call us to tell us how you stuck it out and eventually broke through.

That would make us very happy.

One book can change everything.

Interested in writing a book of your own?

Get our <u>FREE</u> checklist covering every step of the writing, publishing and book marketing process at:

<u>MillionDollarBookFormula.com</u>

Want to Learn More?

Save $200 on our popular Million Dollar Book Formula online course!

Delivered in a series of video training modules, the Million Dollar Book Formula course will teach you:

- To identify your book's true purpose
- The easiest strategies for organizing and writing your manuscript
- Core marketing concepts to give your book the best chance for success
- How to design your cover so it sells (and avoid designs that will kill sales)
- The most important strategies for becoming an Amazon bestseller (and what not to waste your time on)
- The mindset you must have for the greatest chances for success and how to employ long-term marketing strategies that don't have to break your bank
- How to transition from a single book to a series and a highly-profitable "brand"
- A collection of our most treasured secrets for book promotion that few people ever do
- And much, much more!

To receive your $200 discount off the regular price of the course, use code: <u>MDBFBOOK</u>

One book can change everything. Maybe it's time to write yours!

What Others Are Saying...

"When I finished the rough draft of **The Connector's Way**, *I asked Richard and Andrea if they'd be willing to read it and get their thoughts. To be honest, I thought the book was finished—all I wanted was confirmation that it was good to go. That isn't what I got. What I got was much more valuable.*

In a one-hour recorded teleconference, Richard and Andrea gave me three pieces of advice that made a huge difference in the book's success. I know this because many of the people who have bought the book have made comments about the exact things Richard and Andrea encouraged me to change. And the proof is in the sales. This past year, we sold over 10,000 copies of **The Connector's Way**... *received 184 reviews on Amazon, 93 percent of which are 5-Star... and the book has served as the launch-off point for a very lucrative speaking career. I shudder to think about how things might have turned out without their valuable advice."*

-Patrick Galvin, Author, ***The Connector's Way***

"We recently had our book published by Richard Fenton & Andrea Waltz's new publishing company, Success in 100 Pages, and wow—what a great experience! With their guidance every step of the way and our established platform, our book hit #1 in multiple categories on Amazon—and it's still a Top 10 bestseller months later. If you need someone to help you write, publish, and market a book, we highly recommend you work with Richard and Andrea. They know what they're doing."

— Ray and Jessica Higdon, Co-authors, ***Freakishly Effective Social Media for Network Marketing***

More Students Testimonials...

"The Million Dollar Book Formula course was filled with reasonable, practical measures to self-publish my book. It felt like we sat down to Saturday brunch with Richard and Andrea while they shared their most useful tools, experiences, and advice. I ended the program believing I can do this without drowning in the ocean of all possible options." – **Shelley W.**

"Thank you for this fantastic course! It was exactly what I was looking for and a great value for the breadth of material that you covered. I appreciate that you were so open about your many experiences, both good and bad, and that you provided resources and interviews with other successful self-published authors. I highly recommend this course to anyone interested in self-publishing a book." – **Rosemary R.**

"Before I took this course, I thought I knew what it took to write and publish a successful book, but this course was eye opening and showed me how many of the steps I was missing. When I write and publish my book it will be much more successful because of what I learned from this course and will apply. The course was well worth 10 times what it cost me and if you're serious about writing a book you can't afford not to take it".
– **Steve L.**

"I've just finished Richard and Andrea's Million Dollar Book Formula coaching course—wow, so much information and value! They cover all aspects in great detail, so you know exactly what you should be doing to maximize the chances. From the cover design and headline to creating all the content inside and onto the marketing and promoting your book. I may have to go through it 2 or 3 times, there is so much valuable content, I don't want to miss any." – **Richard E.**

About the Authors

Richard Fenton and Andrea Waltz have been writing and self-publishing books for 20 years. After quitting their corporate jobs, they decided to launch their speaking and training company by self-publishing. With no experience, contacts or large financial war chest, they learned everything they needed and managed to pull it off. That first book, *Unlocking the Secrets of Retail Magic,* sold in excess of 40,000 copies, direct to clients and readers, without ever being in a traditional bookstore.

A couple years later, in 2000, they wrote and published the book they are most well-known for (*Go for No!*) which has sold over 400,000 copies and been translated into 9 languages. The book has been among the top 20 best-sellers on Amazon.com on multiple sub-lists for nearly a decade, having hit #1 multiple times.

After writing the book, they created an entire business and brand based on the *Go for No!* strategy including speaking, training, coaching, physical training products, online courses, and more. Today they have a significant social media following and are acknowledged as the go-to experts when it comes to helping people overcome fears of failure, rejection, and the word, No.

Their journey to self-publishing success was not easy and they made a ton of painful mistakes along the way. But all the work and failures paid off. By building a business around their short books, Richard and Andrea created a lifestyle most people only dream of. But most of all, their business has allowed them to do what they love most, which for them is speaking and writing.

Now, they want the same level of freedom they've enjoyed to be yours, too!

Made in the USA
Columbia, SC
08 March 2020